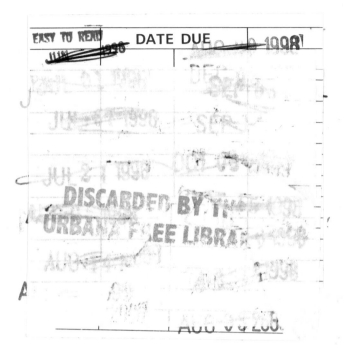

D1065420

A NOTE TO PARENTS

Reading Aloud with Your Child
Research shows that reading books aloud is the single most valuable support parents can provide in helping children learn to read.

- Be a ham! The more enthusiasm you display, the more your child will enjoy the book.
- Run your finger underneath the words as you read to signal that the print carries the story.
- Leave time for examining the illustrations more closely; encourage your child to find things in the pictures.
- Invite your youngster to join in whenever there's a repeated phrase in the text.
- Link up events in the book with similar events in your child's life.
- If your child asks a question, stop and answer it. The book can be a means to learning more about your child's thoughts.

Listening to Your Child Read Aloud
The support of your attention and praise is absolutely crucial to your child's continuing efforts to learn to read.

- If your child is learning to read and asks for a word, give it immediately so that the meaning of the story is not interrupted. DO NOT ask your child to sound out the word.
- On the other hand, if your child initiates the act of sounding out, don't intervene.
- If your child is reading along and makes what is called a miscue, listen for the sense of the miscue. If the word "road" is substituted for the word "street," for instance, no meaning is lost. Don't stop the reading for a correction.
- If the miscue makes no sense (for example, "horse" for "house"), ask your child to reread the sentence because you're not sure you understand what's just been read.
- Above all else, enjoy your child's growing command of print and make sure you give lots of praise. *You are your child's first teacher — and the most important one. Praise from you is critical for further risk-taking and learning.*

— Priscilla Lynch
Ph.D., New York University
Educational Consultant

ISBN 0-590-69767-6

Text copyright © 1997 by Tchin.
Illustrations copyright © 1997 by Carolyn Ewing.
All rights reserved. Published by Scholastic Inc.
HELLO READER!, CARTWHEEL BOOKS, and the CARTWHEEL BOOKS logo are registered trademarks of Scholastic Inc.

Library of Congress Cataloging-in-Publication Data

Tchin.
    Rabbit's wish for snow / by Tchin ; illustrated by Carolyn Ewing.
       p.   cm.— (Hello reader! Level 2)
    Summary: Retells the Native American folktale which explains how rabbits came to look as they do today.
    ISBN 0-590-69767-6 (alk. paper)
    [1. Indians of North America — Folklore. 2. Rabbits — Folklore.
3. Folklore — North America.] I. Ewing, C. S., ill. II. Title.
III. Series.
PZ8.1.T22Rab   1996
398.24'529322'08997— dc20   96-24746
                                         CIP
                                         AC

12 11 10 9 8 7 6 5   7 8 9/9 0 1 2/0
Printed in the U.S.A.   24
First Scholastic printing, January 1997

Rabbit's Wish for Snow

A Native American Legend

▲▲▲▲▲▲▲▲▲

by Tchin
Illustrated by Carolyn Ewing

Hello Reader!—Level 2

SCHOLASTIC INC.

Cartwheel
·B·O·O·K·S·®

New York   Toronto   London   Auckland   Sydney

Long ago,
rabbits were not
as they are today.
Rabbits had long bushy tails
and long straight arms
and long straight legs.

Winter had passed.
The snows had gone.
Rabbit was out playing.
He saw young shoots
high up in a tree.
He wanted to eat
those young shoots.
But rabbits, even then,
were not good tree climbers.

Rabbit also wanted to play
in the snow.
But there was no snow.
Then he remembered
what Grandma had said.

*If you wish for something
hard enough,
it could happen.*
And so Rabbit danced
and sang.

Oh, I wish it would snow.
I wish it would snow.
I wish the snow would
come down
so I could play.
Oh, how I wish it would snow.
And it started to snow
just a little bit.

And Rabbit was so excited
that he danced even harder
and he sang his song
even stronger.

Oh, how I wish it would snow.
Oh, how I wish it would snow
so I could play in the snow.
Oh, I wish it would snow.

And the snow started to fall
as big as feathers.

And the snow climbed
high up the tree.
And Rabbit was able to eat
some of those young shoots
in the tree.

Oh, Rabbit was so happy
to eat the shoots
from the tree.
Now he could rest.
And he fell asleep.

The next morning
the sun came up.
Rabbit looked around.
All the snow had melted.

Rabbit wanted to go home,
but now he was high
in that tree.
And as you know,
rabbits are not good
tree climbers.

Holding on with his tail,
Rabbit leaned over.
He looked down to the ground
and he wondered how
he was going to get out
of the tree.
And as he leaned over,
there was a big snap.

Rabbit broke his tail,
and fell out of that tree!

When Rabbit crashed
to the ground,
he landed on his face
and split his lip.
And Rabbit broke his arms and legs.

So now all Rabbit's grandchildren
have short tails.
And now all Rabbit's grandchildren
have split lips.
And now all Rabbit's grandchildren
have bent arms and legs.

And if you look at a willow tree,
you may see a rabbit's tail.